Poems for the Soul

Susan M. Werner
Compiled by Fr. Mark Goring, CC

The soul of a poet,
Is different I'm told,
Born of the blessings,
Of cherishing His word.
Poems are the altar,
Their rhythm my joy,
Each with a cadence,
For me to employ,
Receiving a message,
Meant to be shared,
With subtle reminders,
Of how deeply He cared.
I welcome all readers,
To read and to glean,
How these verses touch you,
And what each may mean.

Susan M. Werner

A poem appears in my inbox,

From someone I do not know.

Oh no!

Too many emails already,

I'm about to click "delete."

But I notice it's only a few short verses.

Maybe I'll glance at the first line or two.

Simple, beautiful, gentle;

And so I read on...

And now my soul is a little more peaceful.

Wow! What a wonderful poem.

The next day, there's another poem in my inbox.

And now Susan and I are good friends.

Fr. Mark Goring, CC

You kissed me on the forehead,
Then sent me on my way,
As I began to live my life,
You gave me words to say,
You sprinkled stardust in my hands,
They were Your words of Love,
You breathed the gift of prose in me,
A blessing from above.
The only thing You ask of me,
Is not to keep it as my own,
This precious gift I've come to love
You've given as a loan.
I pray, Dear Lord, I'll treasure it,
This gift so rare and dear,
And, every time I share a verse,
I'll feel that You are near.

How great Thou Art, how small I am,

Your grandeur humbles me,

Gentle waters cleanse my soul,

You softly set me free.

Love alone shall purify,

I stand in hope and awe,

Thank you, Lord, for Grace received,

I prayed, You came, I saw.

Change is hard,
I must confess,
With God's sweet grace,
We try our best,
Selfishness gets in the way,
We yearn to have the final say.
Everyone must surely find,
The way of love,
Is to be kind,
He wills for us to ease our grasp,
For things of earth,
Aren't meant to last.

They left from cities, farms and towns,
Folks like you and me,
Service was the call each heard,
A love to keep all free.
Some were lost, others returned,
The call was just the same,
Pray for healing of their wounds,
Remember why they came...
On fields afar as battles raged,
Precious blood was shed,
Injuries of many types,
Harmed body, heart and head.
Remember who and Whose you are,
Give thanks for every breath,
Freedom bears a special cross,
Give thanks for we've been blessed.

As a firm believer,
Everything is Grace,
Every random circumstance,
Shall find its rightful place.
How He loves to please us,
To move us beyond fear,
Gently He will guide us,
His protection is so dear.

Our paths may have been different,
The call has been the same,
His voice has echoed in our hearts,
He has called us each by name.
Circumstances shape our lives,
Our choices different too,
May His love remain the bond,
That ties the "me" to you.

May you deeply know, my friend,
How many lives you've touched,
May you deeply feel His love,
You are treasured very much.
May you seek and always find,
His heart that's wise and true,
May no regret steal your peace,
He blesses all you do.

He knows you need some coaxing,
To begin another day,
The sun will do the wooing,
To start you on the way.
He knows your sleepy senses,
Need to come alive,
A whisper from cool water,
Will help your spirit thrive.
He knows your love of color,
Thus flowers spring to greet
He knows because He made you,
Amid wonder you shall meet...
Love.

A friend who always seeks to give,
Regardless of the cost,
Who waits with endless patience,
Seeking those who may be lost.
A friend who looks beyond the flaws,
And only sees the good,
Then gently soothes the troubled soul,
Just as a best friend should.

The carefree days of childhood,
Whisper to my heart,
You caution to go deeper...
Where is it that I start?
Do I scale the mountaintops,
Or rest in meadowlands
How is it you'll remake me,
Please help me understand.
You know how I lack courage,
Or, perhaps that's not the case,
Bolster me through wisdom,
Kindly lead me to a place...
Of surrender.

Remake me, Lord, and purify,
My heart seems dense as mud,
Soften it with streams of grace,
And blessings from above.
The perfect Craftsman Who You are,
Will keep me on the wheel,
To shape me in Your image,
Yes, I am Yours to heal.

The impossible becomes possible,
As Faith and Hope unite,
Your dreams become reality,
When you cling to what is right.
How He loves to make Himself,
The focus of your day,
Through subtle, clear reminders,
Within the words you pray.

If today you hear His voice,
Harden not your heart,
Look beyond what pleases you....
Become the better part...
A person who annoys you,
Becomes a source of Grace,
The Lord resides in every one,
Transcending time and place.

His tone is soft and joyful,
Likened to the breeze,
Tossing bits of wisdom,
Which land where'er He please.
The impact leaves you breathless,
As such is His intent,
He reminds you of your dignity,
Which you know is heaven sent.

Will you trust your weaknesses,

To become a source for good,

Transformation is His role,

As no man ever could.

Compassion is His offering,

Love and mercy flow,

Welcome He who loves you,

In ways you're yet to know.

My personal view of heaven is:

I'll slide down a rainbow,

And dance in a cloud,

Then swing on a bright star,

As all laugh out loud,

I'll kneel down before You,

And write You a poem,

My heart will be bursting,

I'll know I've come home.

During every precious moment,

That merge to shape a life,

Many eyes are watching you,

Protecting you from strife,

Troubles come; they always do,

Be assured that all is well,

Angels are protecting you,

Allow them to gently dwell,

Within your heart... welcome them,

Such is their cherished role,

The Father made them just for you,

So you may better know...

Him.

It can't be borrowed,
Bought or sold,
Redeemed at any price,
Is dispensed for just the asking,
To the naughty and the nice.
Size and shape it matters not,
Bequeathed to young and old,
With value indescribable,
More precious than pure gold.
A supply that knows no limits,
Ask and you receive,
The only thing required,
Is trust Him and believe...
In unconditional Love.

I ponder what You see in me,
When I feel worn and spent,
I sigh when viewing memories,
How quickly those years went.
Then I feel a gentle nudge,
There is something I must do,
A silent prayer says it all,
Lord, I resemble You!

All you need is what you have,
No need to look beyond,
Renew your mind with simple Truth,
That's where Your love is found...
Nestled in the commonplace,
Competing is for naught...
His gift is for the asking,
Perhaps we just forgot.

No need to be a hero,
Don't strive to do too much,
Your kindness is so precious,
And will always be enough.
Make each act a prayer,
Flowing from your heart,
Simplicity is everything,
And is the better part...
Of life.

Mary and her Joseph,
Were just like you and me,
Will you welcome Jesus,
Into your family?
Will you watch in wonder,
As He grows inside of you.
Will you listen to His words,
As He gently speaks with you?
You are also chosen,
For kinship with them all,
All it takes is patience,
In responding to His call...
They did.

Be careful in your word and deed,

You have so much to give,

Every little sacrifice,

May help another live.

Become a willing shepherd,

To all who come your way,

Charity should be the rule,

You follow every day.

Don't worry about tomorrow,
Rather pray to persevere,
Fortify your weakened will,
With words He's sure to hear.
Your unknowing becomes prayer,
As you slowly place control,
Into the Hands who made you,
Trust that He loves you so.

He sets the sky ablaze at night,
As sunlight gives a nod,
Tiny stars wink and blink,
How wondrous is God!
Wise and gentle are His ways,
Coaxing all who dwell below,
To raise their eyes to heaven,
For His otherworldly show.

At times the shadows beckon,

Toward a peacefulness within,

With time of calm reflection,

Sweet dreams may now begin.

Say a little prayer,

Savor every word,

Allow your heart the privilege,

To welcome your dear Lord.

The truth shall always be the truth,
A lie will be a lie,
Christ will always be the One,
Whose purpose was to die...
To save the world by being born,
In a humble circumstance,
Your search starts at the manger,
Please give Him just a chance...
To Love you.

Tabernacle

A golden box I visit,
Often through the day,
No appointment is required,
Nor special words to say.
He welcomes every visit,
This friend I've come to know,
The blessed Lord resides there,
He helps my Faith to grow.
And waits... And listens.

As humans we're conflicted,
The messages are skewed,
This world is brash and angry,
We feel beaten, worn and used.
There is another message,
From One greater than the earth,
Come prepare your weary heart,
To welcome Jesus' birth.

God uses broken people,
We know this to be true,
As we accept our weaknesses,
His love comes pouring through.
He is our ark to stay afloat,
Our calm on angry seas,
Noah, Moses, Peter, too,
Were just like you and me...
Rejoice, He is coming!

Are you just a bit confused,

Do you need to pause and rest,

Someone always near to You,

Will help relieve your stress.

Take a chance to ease the grip,

On what weighs on your mind,

Prayer gives the hope you seek,

I leave no soul behind...

Your Jesus

Nothing ventured,

Nothing gained,

Refined by Grace,

I have no shame.

Expecting naught,

Receiving all,

I heard Your voice...

Answered Your call.

Take a chance,

Expand your view,

Something grand,

Waits for you.

One little step,

Is all it takes,

Answers come,

To he who waits.

Before I scale the mountain top,
To savor all I see,
I first must walk the valley,
To find the depth of me.
Ignorance is never bliss,
I've learned this to be true,
Embracing my humanity,
Leads my heart to You.

You are a hero dear to me,

A sinner who heard God's call,

Struck by God's almighty hand,

You became a voice for all,

You suffered but you persevered,

Your words became the guide

Inspiring us through streams of Grace,

That move us deep inside.

Pray for me, beloved Paul,

That I may be like you,

Rich in Faith, steeped in Love,

With a heart that's always true.

St. Michael you surround me,
With your shield of cobalt blue,
Watching and protecting,
All I say and do.
Your sword points at the ready,
Warning any who come near,
Not to touch or harm me,
It's you they'll come to fear.
That sword tip now encircles me,
I know you will defend,
My life in every circumstance,
From beginning to the end.
I honor you for loving me,
This and every day,
I sing your praises in my heart,
To you I always pray.

Oh, great archangel, Raphael,
You will heal and lend a hand,
As I navigate this earth,
In search of peaceful land.
God promised you would guide me,
How needy I can be,
It seems at times my Faith is weak,
In trusting Truths I cannot see.
Please lead me on this journey,
Help me complete my race,
I long to rest in God's strong arms,
Humbly walk me to that place.

Gabriel,

You are the very strength of God,

Wrapped in angelic form,

It was you who spoke to Mary,

Announcing God's Son would be born.

You asked her for a selfless yes,

She would bear The Sacred Child,

She searched her heart, gave Him her will,

For she was humble, meek and mild.

With her yes the world would change,

God's Son absolved our shame,

Your simple message rang with Truth,

As you spoke her blessed name...

Hail Mary full of Grace!

Trust Me were the words He spoke,

The moment...hushed and still,

Listen closely to your heart,

As you discern My will.

You must not trust the things of earth,

They were never meant to last,

Release all worry to my hands,

Do not dwell upon the past.

He said,

It's time to spread those nimble wings,

And float beneath My eyes,

I am always watching you,

This should be of no surprise.

My precious one, He softly spoke,

Through adventure you will grow,

I am the lift beneath your wings,

This truth you'll come to know.

I'm grateful for the loving hands,
That touch my life each day,
I'm thankful for each prayer said,
They help me on my way.
I'm hopeful I have done my best,
In all ways big and small,
To comprehend Your sacrifice,
Is the greatest Joy of all.

As a child when I "felt" hurt,
I stuffed those feelings in a bag,
It went unseen but nonetheless,
Some days it made me sad.
With age the bag got bigger, too,
It made my poor heart ache,
Dragging all that stuff around,
Seemed more than I could take.
When I knew You were my friend,
I gave my bag away,
You gladly took all that I gave,
I softly heard You say...
You are Mine.

Strength resting in humility,

Responding to His gentle call,

Learning how to take a walk,

Basking in the glory of it all.

Becoming singular of mind with Him,

Uniting two hearts now as one,

Receiving salvation through the mystery,

Who is His Sacred Son.

Pray for all conflicted souls,
They know not what they do,
Be a vessel of forgiveness,
The world's in need of you.
Pray you may be faithful,
Regardless of the cost,
Pray for all our brothers,
Then humbly bear your cross.

At daybreak I began to stir,
My eyes not quite awake,
In my heart I sensed a calm,
With a willingness to take...
A chance that Faith will always be,
The anchor of my soul,
Thank you, Lord, for showing me,
The ways I need to grow.

There's a second journey we must take,
Beyond the dreams of youth,
A journey deep within the soul,
Where we come to learn the truth.
This path is sure to test the will,
Self-knowledge is our goal,
Cling to Faith and forge ahead,
He shows where we must go.

I love to spend my time with You,
My heart You know so well,
The little secrets that I share,
In Faith You'll never tell.
A gentle touch, a loving gaze,
Are mine to softly hold,
I'm grateful, Lord, to be a part,
Of the Greatest Story ever told...
Creation

You came disguised as my own life,
How else could I let You in,
Gently You took all of me,
So my new life would begin.
This life is one of constant change,
It's Your way to help me grow,
Softly You then called to me,
To take a walk I did not know.
I faced a point of no return,
Where Faith and Love entwine,
I was called to be Your masterpiece,
Evolving beautifully with time.

I think I can,

Ok I'll try,

My eyes are on the goal,

If I fail,

It's not the end,

Perhaps You want to show,

Failure is an option,

Perfection is a myth,

If I hadn't even tried,

There's much I may have missed!

At times I disappoint myself,
Just when I thought I'd move ahead,
Bad habits seem to resurrect,
And I regress instead.
Is this how You show mercy?
How You turn the other cheek?
Does my ambivalence insult you?
Do You love me when I'm weak?
I close my eyes and breathe prayer,
Trusting mercy is the key,
Though I fall I always rise,
Love keeps me twinned with You.

I have failed,
I have confessed ,
Then stepped aside,
You did the rest.
Mercy flowed,
No stains remain,
Healed and whole,
I'm not the same.
My cross is held,
In both my hands,
You are the One,
Who understands.

The Enemy conspires,

Our Father inspires,

The Enemy ensnares,

Our Father cares,

The enemy steals,

Our Father heals,

The Enemy taunts,

Our Father wants...

To give us everything for eternal life with Him.

I began my day, sharp and clean,
My need for order made it so,
Time was planned for each event,
There were places I must go.
Before too long I hit a bump,
I was rocking to and fro,
Worry slowly claimed my thoughts,
There were places yet to go!
His voice displaced the growing angst,
There was something I should know,
Patience always paves the way,
To places He would show...

A morning sun was smiling,
The field seemed dry and spent,
A dandelion dared to rise,
So softly its blooms went...
Carried by the Spirit's breath,
To places close and dear,
Allow your dreams to carry you
Beyond your doubt and fear.

I choose to live in joy this day,
With service as my creed,
Charity shall be the norm,
As I sacrifice each need…
You will be my partner,
Teaching me the words to say,
Renew my mind, Dear Father,
Then lead me on the way,
To Unselfishness.

The earthen jar was emptied,
Its contents long since gone,
Replenishment was manifest,
When Our Savior came along.
This jar was seen as useless,
Till He filled it to the brim,
Resplendent through a miracle,
As a testament to Him.

When you are lost and emptied,
Feeling useless and unkept,
Allow His love to fill your soul,
Then you have surely met...
Abba, Father

The journey you are asked to take,
Is chosen just for you,
Joy and sorrow line the path,
With much you're called to do.
I am the guide you need to trust,
For I shall lead the way,
Redemption manifests itself,
As you softly learn to pray...
Our Father, Who art in heaven

At At dawn's first light,
The mist dispels,
The voice of God,
Has much to tell.
Arise to greet,
Another morn,
First give Him thanks,
You have been born.
Feed your soul,
With grace He gives,
His way is truth,
Then start...to live!

Little one I've watched you,
You appear to be alone,
May I gently ask of you,
The reason why you roam?
Do you think you're different,
A little out of place?
As we walk I'll clear your heart,
Through streams of healing grace.
I promise we'll walk slowly,
We won't go very far,
Then your eyes are open,
To the truth of Whose you are.

Your message is a simple one,

Don't try to get ahead,

Rank is unimportant,

Do your best instead.

Mirror how He lived His life,

Simplicity comes first,

Self-knowledge comes from loving Him,

Then your heart will burst...

With humility

The critic when defensive,
Enjoys to hold his ground,
Forming harsh opinions.
Of everything around.
The One who all should mirror,
Took judgement to the cross,
Come and follow He who Loves,
Regardless of the cost.

Mercy took a hold of me,

Then would not let me go,

Not until I knew the truth,

For He had much to show.

I am God's disciple,

Among the many flawed,

Angry and impatient ,

Before this loving God.

Like Peter I denied Him,

Like James and John I ran,

Like Thomas I have doubted,

Now, I'm clasping Mercy's hand.

For God is my salvation,

To this I will attest,

Humbly I gaze upward,

His Mercy does the rest.

Welcome to the brotherhood of man!

I'm not on a fast lane,
I've given Him the lead,
Others may go faster,
He knows my perfect speed.
Patience is a virtue,
I'm praying to possess,
In His eyes I'm faithful,
Persevering is Success!

Will you join His army,
To recruit the other souls,
Who hesitate from weakness,
To take the path He chose,
Humility shall be your sword,
Charity...your shield,
Prayer is your battle cry,
In Faith... you will not yield.

Let's walk within His garden,
There's much to be explored,
Amid the scents and whispers,
You find our loving Lord.
The arrogant won't find it,
The humble walk the path,
By bearing all their crosses,
They're finding home... at last.

My mind was full of mischief ,
I'd give the world a shout,
Life would be just perfect,
Isn't that what it's about?
When I saw the simple path,
And no flowers lined the way,
I was rendered speechless,
I found beauty in each day.

I am just a normal person,
Who is growing in her Faith,
Many people come to me,
To help put things in place.
I could write a novel,
About what I've done and seen,
God has slowly shaped me,
He's always come between...
What could have soon destroyed me,
I've felt His loving hand,
My prayer becomes fruitful,
Because He understands...
Me.

He whispers...

I see the pensive look you wear,

It's failure that you fear,

Never stifle willingness,

Your mind I wish to clear.

Everyone who follows Me,

Will stumble now and then,

Success is measured in My eyes,

By those who try again...

And again.

You don't have every answer,
A walk may clear your mind,
Questions become prayers,
As you leave each doubt behind.
Struggle is apparent,
Your footsteps seem to pound,
Slowly tranquil whisperings,
Become the Sacred sound.

As I arise from peaceful rest,
One truth will come to me,
Every moment I've been watched,
By one I cannot see.
A special mission was embraced,
For such was Your design,
Gratefully I offer praise,
For this angel who is mine.

You'll never know the lives you've touched,
Or how the world was changed,
Because you gave your all to Him,
And never were ashamed...
To fail.

I planned to write my story,
Oh, it would be so grand,
Your gentle touch relaxed the grip,
Of the pen within my hand.
Your loving stroke erased my need,
To embellish what was real,
You arrived to speak the truth,
In the perfect way to heal...
Me

Lord

Please walk me through my desert,

I've wandered far too long,

Bless me with sustaining grace,

As I raise my heart in song.

You have sought me everywhere.

So many years have passed,

Relationship is what I seek,

I have found my way at last!

I want to reach and touch Your hand,
To trust that You are real,
I want to find You next to me,
As I bend my knee to kneel.
I want to know deep in my soul,
You truly died for me,
I want to comfort all Your pain,
For Your passion I must see.
Only when I grow in Faith,
Will I learn just who I am,
You are my Shepherd guarding me,
A wayward little lamb.

You packed a bag full of regret,
Stuffed worry in there, too,
Then headed off in solitude,
And found Him watching you.
Smiling ... He took everything,
For He now owned your heart,
To share a deeper journey,
You had shared the weakest part..
Of your humanity.

Ordinary people,
Called to do His work,
Hand in hand in brotherhood,
Their duties.... never shirked.
Oh, to know the battles,
These people surely fought,
Masked behind a smiling face,
Through what could not be
bought.
LOVE.

Where were You when I rebelled,
Certain others did not see,
How I struggled with myself,
What would become of me?
Courage came through someone else,
Who listened and observed,
Responding to a silent prayer,
Without a spoken word.

Pause to take a gentle breath,
Each thought becomes a prayer,
Situations always change,
The Lord is everywhere.
Maintain a focus on the One,
Who holds you in His hand,
Loving fingers stroke your heart,
As you come to understand...
Conversion.

At times my world seems upside down,
That I'm clinging by a thread,
Another world awaits me though,
So I trust in You instead.
Upside down or rightside up,
It matters not to me,
Your mighty Hand holds everything,
For all is meant to be...
Yours.

Our paths have not been crossing,

How I've been missing you!

This door cannot be opened,

I know the things you do.

The latch is on the inside,

Do you hear my gentle knock,

If you let me enter,

Heart to heart we'll talk.

Your Jesus.

Throughout His earthly ministry,
Questions were addressed,
Who and how and why were asked,
And though they tried to guess,
This band of men He carefully chose,
Were blinded to the plan,
Until the Spirit made them see,
Their roles in saving man.

His thought became reality,

The day you were designed,

Fashioned oh so splendidly,

A gift to humankind.

Perfect in your weaknesses,

Through Grace your soul shall thrive,

Regardless of the circumstance,

Give praise... you are alive!

Wealth beyond your wildest dreams,
A castle large and grand,
Clothes and jewels of plenitude,
Yet some don't understand.
The priceless gift I offer,
Is an endless stream of grace,
Gaze upon My countenance,
Which nothing can replace...
You are loved.

I saw you sitting on the ledge,
With nothing much to do,
Quietly I chose a place,
So I'd be next to you.
Let's talk a bit of simple joys,
I love to see you smile,
It comforts Me to be with you,
I'm going to stay a while.

Always in a hurry,
I chose to stop and pray,
Nothing grand and verbose,
Just thoughts I longed to say,
My angel sent them heavenward,
Knowing where they need to go,
God's perfect Love expanded them,
So I may slowly grow...
My Faith.

She thought no one would notice,
As she dared to join the crowd,
Approaching seemed impossible,
Voices were so loud.
Silence was her option,
She stretched to touch His cloak,
Immediately she understood,
For heart to heart they spoke...
Of healing through forgiveness.

The water jugs were empty,
She approached the well to fill,
Earthen jars with sustenance,
Being careful not to spill...
A stranger paused to greet her,
His words would touch her mind,
Her superficial life was changed,
As she left the past behind.

Take a peek inside yourself,
I'll give you just a glimpse,
Dare you love the image,
Or will you turn and wince?
I alone can read your heart,
For every thought is known,
Embrace your true uniqueness,
You are Mine alone.

I'm sitting in my quiet place,
The air is light and still,
Everything seems perfect!
In accordance with Your will.
A song arises in my heart,
This lovely joyful tune,
Floats among the shimmering clouds,
On a splendid afternoon.
Praise God!

Share with me your story,
Who do you think I am,
In truth I am your Shepherd,
You are my precious lamb.
Rise and spend the day with Me,
There's much we shall explore,
Through my eyes you'll see a world,
You may have missed before.

Manufactured by Amazon.ca
Bolton, ON

40018885R00055